Dog Wit

DOG WIT

Copyright © Summersdale Publishers Ltd, 2012

Illustrations by Ian Baker

Summersdale Publishers Ltd
46 West Street
Chichester
West Sussex
PO19 1RP
UK

www.summersdale.com

Printed and bound by CPI Group (UK) Ltd, Croydon, CR0 4YY

ISBN: 978-1-84953-316-4

Substantial discounts on bulk quantities of Summersdale books are available to corporations, professional associations and other organisations. For details telephone Summersdale Publishers on (+44-1243-771107), fax (+44-1243-786300) or email (nicky@summersdale.com).

Dog Wit

Quips and Quotes for the Canine-Obsessed

Kate May

Illustrations by Ian Baker

summersdale

Contents

Editor's Note

What have dogs ever done for us? Much more than you'd think, according to everyone from George Bernard Shaw to Agatha Christie, Mark Twain to Marilyn Monroe, and from Lord Byron to Barbara Woodhouse. In fact, dogs are our most faithful friends, which is why the name Fido – Latin for 'I am faithful' – became so popular.

We tend to think they're our most philosophical friends too, although as Merrill Markoe pointed out about the look of existential angst on her crazy canine's face, sometimes 'all he is actually doing is slowly scanning the ceiling for flies'. Our problem is, how do we understand these creatures to whom the whole world is a smell, who spend their days sleeping or bounding around, seemingly without a care in the world?

Of course, this is why we love them – for their joyous exuberance, their unconditional affection and their capacity to listen without talking back. James Herriot commented that animals have more soul than humans, if 'having a soul means being able to feel love and loyalty and gratitude'. So who cares if your pooch has no interest in doing what it's told? As long as these four-legged friends share our homes, we'll be barking mad about them.

Maybe you wish your dog could talk back to you but really you know that everything that needs to be said between the two of you has already been understood, through hugs, woofs, wags and walks. So have a good scratch and enjoy this witty collection of quips and quotes on the delights of living in the doghouse.

MAN'S BEST FRIEND

It often happens
that a man is more
humanely related to
a cat or dog than to
any human being.

Henry David Thoreau

If you eliminate
smoking and gambling,
you will be amazed
to find that almost
all an Englishman's
pleasures can be,
and mostly are,
shared by his dog.

George Bernard Shaw

Dogs love company. They place it first in their short list of needs.

J. R. Ackerley

When a man's best friend is his dog, that dog has a problem.

Edward Abbey

Outside of a dog, a book is a man's best friend. Inside of a dog it's too dark to read.

Groucho Marx

For company I have my dogs;
for words, my books.

Robert Coane

＊

Our dogs will love and admire the
meanest of us, and feed our colossal
vanity with their uncritical homage.

Agnes Repplier

＊

... amid all the forms of life that
surround us, not one, excepting the
dog, has made an alliance with us.

Maurice Maeterlinck

A dog wags its tail with its heart.

Anonymous

I think we are drawn to dogs
because they are the uninhibited
creatures we might be if we
weren't certain we knew better.

George Bird Evans

Few delights can equal
the mere presence of one
whom we trust utterly.

George MacDonald

No animal I know of can
consistently be more of a friend
and companion than a dog.

Stanley Leinwoll

Everyone knows that dogs
lick the people they like.

Suzanne Clothier

DOGGY DIALOGUE

If animals could speak, the dog would be a blundering outspoken fellow.

Mark Twain

When most of us talk to our dogs, we tend to forget they're not people.

Julia Glass

❖

He is the one 'person' to whom I can talk without the conversation coming back to war.

Dwight D. Eisenhower on his Scottie dog

❖

If dogs could talk, perhaps we would find it as hard to get along with them as we do with people.

Karel Čapek

If dogs talked, one
of them would be
president by now.

Dean Koontz

[Dogs] never talk about
themselves but listen to you while
you talk about yourself, and
keep up an appearance of being
interested in the conversation.

Jerome K. Jerome

The reason a dog has so many
friends is that he wags his
tail instead of his tongue.

Anonymous

No one appreciates the
very special genius of your
conversation as the dog does.

Christopher Morley

An animal's eyes have the power
to speak a great language.

Martin Buber

If dogs could talk, it would take a
lot of the fun out of owning one.

Andy Rooney

Say something idiotic and nobody
but a dog politely wags his tail.

Virginia Graham

A dog can express
more with his tail
in seconds than
his owner can
express with his
tongue in hours.

Anonymous

PUPPY LOVE

Whoever said you
can't buy happiness
forgot little puppies.

Gene Hill

Puppies are nature's remedy for
feeling unloved, plus numerous
other ailments of life.

Richard Allan Palm

———

When a puppy takes fifty
catnaps in the course of the day,
he cannot always be expected
to sleep the night through.

Albert Payson Terhune

———

Happiness is a warm puppy.

Charles M. Schulz

A puppy plays with every
pup he meets, but an old
dog has few associates.

Josh Billings

Buy a pup and your money
will buy love unflinching.

Rudyard Kipling

Oh the saddest of sights
in a world of sin
Is the little lost pup with
his tail tucked in.

Arthur Guiterman, from 'Little Lost Pup'

When you feel lousy, puppy therapy is indicated.

Sara Paretsky

Of all the things I miss from veterinary practice, puppy breath is one of the most fond memories.

Dr Tom Cat

The best way to get a puppy is to beg for a baby brother—and they'll settle for a puppy every time.

Winston Pendleton

A puppy is but a dog, plus high spirits, and minus common sense.

Agnes Repplier

No symphony orchestra ever played music like a two-year-old girl laughing with a puppy.

Bern Williams

THE TRUTH ABOUT CATS AND DOGS

It's funny how dogs and cats know the inside of folks better than other folks do.

Eleanor H. Porter

Everyone should have a dog that will worship him and a cat that will ignore him.

Dereke Bruce on keeping one's
importance in perspective

Cat's motto: No matter what you've done wrong, always try to make it look like the dog did it.

Anonymous

Women and cats will do as they please, and men and dogs should relax and get used to the idea.

Robert A. Heinlein

I care not for a man's religion whose
dog and cat are not the better for it.

Abraham Lincoln

———◦———

A house without either a cat or a
dog is the house of a scoundrel.

Portuguese proverb

———◦———

Cats are smarter than dogs.
You can't get eight cats to
pull a sled through snow.

Jeff Valdez

Dogs eat. Cats dine.

Ann Taylor

———•———

Charley has no interest in cats
whatever, even for chasing purposes.

John Steinbeck on his poodle Charley

———•———

[I am a] dog man, and all felines
can tell this at a glance - a
sharp, vindictive glance.

James Thurber

The cat is the mirror
of his human's mind...
the dog mirrors his
human's physical
appearance.

Winifred Carriere

The dog is mentioned
in the Bible eighteen
times – the cat
not even once.

W. E. Farbstein

IT'S A DOG'S LIFE

What does a dog
do on his day off?
He can't lie around
– that's his job.

George Carlin

A door is what a
dog is perpetually on
the wrong side of.

Ogden Nash

Dogs lead a nice life. You never see a dog with a wristwatch.

George Carlin

The greatest fear dogs know is... that you will not come back when you go out the door without them.

Stanley Coren

Dogs feel very strongly that they should always go with you in the car.

Dave Barry

The dog lives for the day, the hour, even the moment.

Robert Falcon Scott

If a dog's prayers were answered, bones would rain from the sky.

Proverb

A DOG'S DINNER

A dog in the kitchen
asks for no company.

French proverb

The dogs eat of the crumbs which
fall from their masters' table.

Matthew 15:27

Never chain your dogs
together with sausages.

John Berger

Ever see a dog eat sushi? He just
sniffs it and says 'I don't think so'.

Billiam Coronel

They serve us in return for scraps. It is without doubt the best deal man has ever made.

Roger Caras

My pit bull was choking on his dinner. I squeezed his stomach and the neighbour's cat shot right out.

Scott Wood

A dog desires affection more than its dinner. Well – almost.

Charlotte Gray

The ideal dog food would be a
ration that tastes like a postman.

Anonymous

———•———

He claims that he genuinely believed
it to be a table meant for dogs.

**Jean Little, whose dog has only ever
stolen food from a coffee table**

———•———

A dog that runs after two
bones catches neither.

English proverb

Every time I go near the
stove, the dog howls.

Phyllis Diller

They have dog food for constipated
dogs. If your dog is constipated,
why screw up a good thing?

David Letterman

THE FAIRER SPECIES

But never yet the
dog our country fed,
Betrayed the
kindness or forgot
the bread.

Edward Bulwer-Lytton

The more I see of man,
the better I like dogs.

Madame Roland

A dog owns nothing, yet
is seldom dissatisfied.

Irish proverb

Dogs are our link to paradise.
They don't know evil or
jealousy or discontent.

Milan Kundera

Character is higher than intellect.

Ralph Waldo Emerson

The average dog is a nicer person
than the average person.

Andy Rooney

The dog is a gentleman; I hope
to go to his heaven, not man's.

Mark Twain

You think dogs will not be in heaven? I tell you, they will be there long before any of us.

Robert Louis Stevenson

Dogs are miracles with paws.

Susan Ariel

Dogs got personality. Personality goes a long way.

Quentin Tarantino

I love dogs. They
live in the moment
and don't care about
anything except
affection and food.

David Duchovny

GENTLE GIANTS

The Lion-Maned
Dog stood, a solid,
motionless mass, in the
middle of the lawn...
squashing the daisies.

Barrie Hawkins, *Twenty Wagging Tales*

Many vets live in more fear of
[hamsters] than they do of any forty-
kilo, highly trained prison guard dog.

Emma Milne, *Tales from the Tail End*

Inside every Newfoundland,
boxer, elkhound and Great
Dane is a puppy longing
to climb on to your lap.

Helen Thomson

Dalmatians are not only superior
to other dogs, they are like all dogs,
infinitely less stupid than men.

Eugene O'Neill

Things that upset
a terrier may pass
virtually unnoticed
by a Great Dane.

Smiley Blanton

The Weimaraner is the Rolls-Royce of the dog world. Or more specifically, the Rolls-Royce Silver Ghost.

Andrew Dilger, *Dash*

The biggest dog has been a pup.

Joaquin Miller

In the dog-eat-dog economy, the Doberman is boss.

Edward Abbey

The Airedale... an unrivalled mixture
of brains and clownish wit, the very
ingredients one looks for in a spouse.

Chip Brown

You can run with the big dogs
or sit on the porch and bark.

Wallace Arnold

Rambunctious, rumbustious,
delinquent dogs become
angelic when sitting.

Dr Ian Dunbar

CANINE CAPERS

The dog was created
specially for children.
He is the god of frolic.

Henry Ward Beecher

I have a dog of Blenheim birth,
With fine long ears and full of mirth;
And sometimes, running
o'er the plain,
He tumbles on his nose:
But quickly jumping up again,
Like lightning on he goes!

John Ruskin

Every boy should have two
things: a dog, and a mother
willing to let him have one.

Anonymous

They motivate us to play,
be affectionate, seek
adventure and be loyal.

Tom Hayden

Scratch a dog
and you'll find a
permanent job.

Franklin P. Jones

A dog is like an eternal Peter Pan,
a child who never grows old.

Aaron Katcher

We don't stop playing because
we grow old; we grow old
because we stop playing.

George Bernard Shaw

Investigators have discovered
that dogs can laugh, which can't
be too big of a surprise.

Tony Snow

In times of joy, all of us wished we
possessed a tail we could wag.

W. H. Auden

All of the animals except for
man know that the principle
business of life is to enjoy it.

Samuel Butler

Love the animals: God has
given them the rudiments of
thought and joy untroubled.

Fyodor Dostoyevsky

WALKIES!

If it wasn't for dogs,
some people would
never go for a walk.

Emily Dickinson

To sit with a dog on a hillside
on a glorious afternoon is
to be back in Eden.

Milan Kundera

Golf seems to be an arduous
way to go for a walk. I prefer
to take the dogs out.

HRH Princess Anne

You can't expect a dog to pass
up a policeman on a bicycle.
It isn't human nature.

P. G. Wodehouse

Hardly any animal can look as deeply disappointed as a dog to whom one says 'No'.

Jeffrey Moussaieff Masson

I looked down at Boogie and he was slouching along with an old biscuit wrapper in his mouth.

Mark Wallington

To be followed home by a stray dog is a sign of impending wealth.

Chinese proverb

They keep you
honest about walking
because when it's
time to go, you
can't disappoint
those little faces.

Wendie Malick

Ever wonder where
you'd end up if you
took your dog for
a walk and never
once pulled back?

Robert Brault

SMALL IS BEAUTIFUL

A chihuahua. They're
good. If you lose
one, just empty
out your purse.

Jean Carroll

It's the dog for lazy people. You don't have to walk it. Just hold it out the window and squeeze.

Anthony Clark on the chihuahua

I'd rather have an inch of a dog than miles of pedigree.

Dana Burnet

Dachshunds... are
already stretched
and pulled to such
a length that a child
cannot do much harm
one way or another.

Robert Benchley on why dachshunds
are ideal for small children

My little dog – a
heartbeat at my feet.

Edith Wharton

The pug is living proof that
God has a sense of humour.

Margo Kaufman

Fox-terriers are born with about
four times as much original
sin in them as other dogs.

Jerome K. Jerome

Even the tiniest poodle is
lionhearted, ready to do anything to
defend home, master, and mistress.

Louis Sabin

Dachshund: A half-a-dog high
and a dog-and-a-half long.

H. L. Mencken

A Pekingese is not a pet dog;
he is an undersized lion.

A. A. Milne

It sometimes takes days, even weeks,
before a dog's nerves tire. In the case
of terriers it can run into months.

E. B. White

From the lowly perspective of a
dog's eyes, everyone looks short.

Chinese proverb

HEEL!

Dogs travel hundreds
of miles during their
lifetime responding
to such commands as
'come' and 'fetch.'

Stephen Baker

Properly trained, a man can
be dog's best friend.

Corey Ford

My Labrador retriever had
a nervous breakdown. I kept
throwing him a boomerang.

Nick Arnette

I now had a Border collie...
with all the training and
innate sheepdogginess of
a rather bored goldfish.

Emma Milne, *Tales from the Tail End*

Dogs like to obey. It
gives them security.

James Herriot

By and large, people who enjoy
teaching animals to roll over will find
themselves happier with a dog.

Barbara Holland

I can train any dog in five minutes. It's
training the owner that takes longer.

Barbara Woodhouse

A dog teaches a boy fidelity, perseverance, and to turn around three times before lying down.

Robert Benchley

Most owners are at length able to teach themselves to obey their dog.

Robert Morley

When a dog runs at you, whistle for him.

Henry David Thoreau

A dog [after being scolded] slinks off into a corner and pretends to be doing a serious self-reappraisal.

Robert Brault

No animal should ever jump up on the dining room furniture unless... he can hold his own in the conversation.

Fran Lebowitz

A well-trained dog
will make no attempt
to share your lunch.
He will just make
you feel... guilty.

Helen Thomson

LEADER OF THE PACK

The hounds all join
in glorious cry,
The huntsman
winds his horn:
And a-hunting
we will go.

Henry Fielding, from 'A-Hunting We Will Go'

Any woman who does not
thoroughly enjoy tramping across
the country on a clear frosty morning
with a good gun and a pair of dogs
does not know how to enjoy life.

Annie Oakley

A hungry dog hunts best.

Lee Trevino

A hungry dog hunts best. A
hungrier dog hunts even better.

Norman Ralph Augustine

If you're not the lead dog,
the view never changes.

Anonymous

———

Who gets the bird, the
hunter or the dog?

John Lewis

———

Cry, 'Havoc!' and let
slip the dogs of war.

William Shakespeare, *Julius Caesar*

Hunger and fear are the only
realities in dog life: an empty
stomach makes a fierce dog.

Robert Falcon Scott

***

Don't think to hunt two
hares with one dog.

Benjamin Franklin

Like a dog, he hunts in dreams...

Alfred, Lord Tennyson, from 'Locksley Hall'

If there was such a thing as a pack of standard poodles, where would they rove to? Bloomingdale's?

Yvonne Clifford

WHAT HAVE DOGS EVER DONE FOR US?

A dog is a bond between strangers.

John Steinbeck

To his dog, every man is Napoleon; hence the constant popularity of dogs.

Aldous Huxley

I am I because my little dog knows me.

Gertrude Stein

My advice to any diplomat who wants to have good press is to have two or three kids and a dog.

Carl Rowan

A dog is the only thing that can mend a crack in your broken heart.

Judy Desmond

One reason a dog can be such a comfort when you're feeling blue is that he doesn't try to find out why.

Anonymous

Has anyone ever had a stroke or a heart attack while cosied up with a pet? I doubt it.

Robert Brault

No one can fully understand
the meaning of love unless
he's owned a dog.

Gene Hill

The only creatures that are
evolved enough to convey pure
love are dogs and infants.

Johnny Depp

No matter how little money and
how few possessions you own,
having a dog makes you rich.

Louis Sabin

There's just something about dogs that makes you feel good. You come home, they're thrilled to see you.

Janet Schnellman

His ears were often the first thing to catch my tears.

Elizabeth Barrett Browning in reference to her cocker spaniel, Flush

There is no
psychiatrist in the
world like a puppy
licking your face.

Ben Williams

DOGGY DEVOTION

I have found that
when you are deeply
troubled, there are
things you get from
the silent devoted
companionship of a
dog that you can get
from no other source.

Doris Day

The one absolutely unselfish friend
that man can have... the one that
never deserts him... is his dog.

George Graham

My dogs forgive anger in me,
the arrogance in me, the brute
in me. They forgive everything
I do before I forgive myself.

Guy de la Valdene

My goal in life is to
become as wonderful
as my dog thinks I am.

Toby Green

[*The Odyssey* is] the story of a man who returned home... and was recognised only by his dog.

Guillermo C. Infante

—◆—

If your dog thinks you're the greatest person in the world, don't seek a second opinion.

Jim Fiebig

—◆—

A dog is the only thing on earth that loves you more than he loves himself.

Josh Billings

Dogs are not our whole life, but they make our lives whole.

Roger Caras

The dog has been esteemed and loved by all the people on earth... for he renders services that have made him man's best friend.

Alfred Barbou

I love a dog. He does nothing for political reasons.

Will Rogers

If ever the world's diplomats and arms negotiators learn the spaniel gaze there will be peace on earth.

Larry Shook

We long for an affection altogether ignorant of our faults. Heaven has accorded this to us in the uncritical canine attachment.

George Eliot

A dog has one aim in life... to bestow his heart.

J. R. Ackerley

DOG LOVERS

Dog lovers are a good
breed themselves.

Gladys Taber

When you and your beloved
dog rely on each other for
nearly everything, your love is
multiplied to epic proportions.

Dianne Phelps

The gift which I am sending you
is called a dog, and is in fact
the most precious and valuable
possession of mankind.

Theodorus Gaza

Most dogs, given the choice, will
actually prefer human company
to other dog company.

John Bradshaw

Dogs have more love than integrity.

Clarence Day

—•—

I think dogs are the most amazing creatures; they give unconditional love... they are the role model for being alive.

Gilda Radner

—•—

The greater love is a mother's; then comes a dog's; then a sweetheart's.

Polish proverb

I have always thought
of a dog lover as a
dog that was in love
with another dog.

James Thurber

I can tell you that I'd rather
be kissed by my dogs than by
some people I've known.

Bob Barker

———

My wife kisses the dog on the lips,
yet she won't drink from my glass.

Rodney Dangerfield

———

Love is the emotion that a woman
feels always for a poodle dog
and sometimes for a man.

George Jean Nathan

Money can buy you a fine dog, but only love can make him wag his tail.

Kinky Friedman

❦

With the exception of women, there is nothing on earth so agreeable or necessary to the comfort of man as the dog.

Edward Jesse

❦

A wet dog is the lovingest.

Ogden Nash

THE DOG MAKETH
THE MAN

The dog represents
all that is best in man.

Etienne Charlet

Whosoever loveth me
loveth my hound.

Sir Thomas More

Who kicks a dog kicks his
own soul towards hell.

Will Judy

A house is not a home
until it has a dog.

Gerald Durrell

Until one has loved an animal, a part
of one's soul remains unawakened.

Anatole France

Any man who does not like dogs
and want them about does not
deserve to be in the White House.

Calvin Coolidge

A watchdog is a dog kept to guard
your home, usually by sleeping
where a burglar would awaken the
household by falling over him.

Anonymous

The point of it is to open
oneself to the possibility of
becoming partly a dog.

Edward Hoagland on how to enjoy dog ownership

You don't really own a dog, you
rent them... you have to be thankful
that you had a long lease.

Joe Garagiola

If you don't own a dog... there may
be something wrong with your life.

Roger Caras

A person who has never
owned a dog has missed a
wonderful part of life.

Bob Barker

A man's soul can be judged by
the way he treats his dog.

Charles Doran

WOOFY WISDOM

All knowledge,
the totality of all
questions and all
answers is contained
in the dog.

Franz Kafka

Charley is a mind-reading dog...
He knows we are going long
before the suitcases come out.

John Steinbeck

———

Dogs are wise. They crawl away into
a quiet corner and lick their wounds...
until they are whole once more.

Agatha Christie

———

Dogs teach us a very important
lesson in life: the mail man
is not to be trusted.

Sian Ford

No philosophers
so thoroughly
comprehend us as
dogs and horses.

Herman Melville

If you think dogs can't count, try putting three dog biscuits in your pocket and then giving Fido only two.

Phil Pastoret

A dog has the soul of a philosopher.

Plato

Dogs and philosophers do
the greatest good and get
the fewest rewards.

Diogenes

[It's] not because she's too
stupid to learn how but because
she's too smart to bother.

**Rick Horowitz on why your dog
might not sit up or roll over**

Number 1 Reason Dogs Do
Not Use Computers...
TrO{gO DsA[M,bN
HyAqR4tDc TgrOo TgYPmE
WeljTyH P;AzWqS,.*

Tom Antion

Who can believe that there is no soul
behind the luminous eyes of a dog?

Theophile Gautier

BITE ME

Every dog is
allowed one bite.

American proverb

I squatted down. Immediately, I
realised that my head was about
level with the dog's teeth.

Barrie Hawkins

———•———

The nose of the bulldog has been
slanted backwards so that he
can breathe without letting go.

Winston Churchill

———•———

The small percentage of dogs
that bite people is monumental
proof that the dog is the most
benign, forgiving creature...

W. R. Koehler

[The dachshund] will give you
the impression that he plans to
convert you into a light snack
between his regular meals.

P. G. Wodehouse

A dog's bark may be worse than his
bite, but everyone prefers his bark.

Anonymous

Dogs don't bite when a growl will do.

Luke Barber and Matt Weinstein

That they may have a little
peace, even the best dogs are
compelled to snarl occasionally.

William Feather

I loathe people who keep dogs.
They are cowards who haven't got
the guts to bite people themselves.

August Strindberg

If this dog do you bite, soon
as out of your bed, take a hair
of the tail the next day.

Ebenezer Cobham Brewer

Animals generally return the
love you lavish on them by
a swift bite in passing – not
unlike friends and wives.

Gerald Durrell

Dogs never bite me. Just humans.

Marilyn Monroe

ONE CAREFUL OWNER

There is no such
thing as a difficult
dog, only an
inexperienced owner.

Barbara Woodhouse

I dressed dear
sweet little Dash
for the second time
after dinner in a
scarlet jacket and
blue trousers.

Queen Victoria on her pet Cavalier
King Charles spaniel

My dog is usually pleased with what I do, because she is not infected with the concept of what I 'should' be doing.

Lonzo Idolswine

If you are a dog and your owner suggests that you wear a sweater... suggest that he wear a tail.

Fran Lebowitz

The difference between friends and pets is that friends we allow into our company, pets we allow into our solitude.

Robert Brault

Acquiring a dog may be the
only opportunity a human ever
has to choose a relative.

Mordecai Siegal

The dog alone, of all brute animals,
has an affection upwards to man.

Samuel Taylor Coleridge

I am as confounded by dogs
as I am indebted to them.

Roger Caras

From the dog's point of view,
his master is an elongated and
abnormally cunning dog.

Mabel Louise Robinson

I've seen a look in dogs' eyes...
and I am convinced that basically
dogs think humans are nuts.

John Steinbeck

My husband and I
are either going to
buy a dog or have
a child. We can't
decide whether to
ruin our carpets
or ruin our lives.

Rita Rudner

CRAZY CANINES

It is fatal to let any dog know that he is funny, for he immediately loses his head and starts hamming it up.

P. G. Wodehouse

I wonder if other dogs think poodles
are members of a weird religious cult.

Rita Rudner

❦

Did you hear about the
dyslexic, agnostic insomniac
who stays up all night wondering
if there really is a Dog?

Anonymous

❦

Did you ever walk into a room and
forget why you walked in? I think
that is how dogs spend their lives.

Sue Murphy

Dogs act exactly the
way we would act if
we had no shame.

Cynthia Heimel

Dogs who chase cars evidently
see them as large, unruly
ungulates badly in need of
discipline and shepherding.

Elizabeth Marshall Thomas

Dogs laugh, but they
laugh with their tails.

Max Eastman

The mere jingle of car keys is
enough to send most any dog into
a whimpering, tail-wagging frenzy.

Jon Winokur

Muzzle a dog and he will bark
out of the other end.

Malcolm Lowry

People are amazed when he gets
up and they suddenly realise they
have been talking to the wrong end.

Elizabeth Jones on her shaggy dog

TOP DOG

I am his Highness'
dog at Kew;
Pray tell me, sir,
whose dog are you?

Alexander Pope

Dogs are animals that poop
in public and you're supposed
to pick it up... Who's the real
master in this relationship?

Anthony Griffin

There is honour in being a dog.

Aristotle

Customer: 'Has this dog
a good pedigree?'
Shop Owner: 'Has he? If that
dog could talk, he wouldn't
speak to either of us.'

Anonymous

Man is rated the highest animal,
at least among all animals who
returned the questionnaire.

Robert Brault

❦

Intelligent dogs rarely want to please
people whom they do not respect.

W. R. Koehler

❦

Dogs, the foremost snobs in
creation, are quick to notice the
difference between a well-clad
and a disreputable stranger.

Albert Payson Terhune

The dog has seldom
been successful in
pulling man up to its
level of sagacity.

James Thurber

Some dogs live for
praise, they look
at you as if to say
'Don't throw balls...
just throw bouquets.'

Jhordis Anderson

Every dog is a lion at home.

Giovanni Torriano

Dogs' lives are too short.
Their only fault, really.

Agnes Sligh Turnbull

THE DIFFERENCE
BETWEEN MEN
AND DOGS

I know at last what
distinguishes
man from animals:
financial worries.

Romain Rolland

A dog is nothing but a furry person.

Anonymous

If you pick up a starving dog and make him prosperous, he will not bite you; that is the principal difference between a dog and a man.

Mark Twain

Dogs are my favourite people.

Richard Dean Anderson

He can't read, can't drive a car,
and has no grasp of mathematics...

John Steinbeck on his poodle Charley

❧

Recollect that the Almighty, who
gave the dog to be companion
of our pleasures and our toils,
hath invested him with a nature
noble and incapable of deceit.

Sir Walter Scott

❧

I have yet to see one completely
unspoiled star, except for
the animals – like Lassie.

Edith Head

... certain dogs I have known will go to heaven, and very, very few persons.

James Thurber

I've been sitting my whole life, and a dog has never looked at me as though he thought I was tricky.

Mitch Hedberg on teaching your dog to sit

You call to a dog and a dog will break its neck to get to you. Dogs just want to please.

Lewis Grizzard

Gratitude: that
quality which the
Canine Mongrel
seldom lacks; which
the Human Mongrel
seldom possesses!

Lion P. S. Rees

BARKING MAD

I went to the dentist.
He said 'Say Aaah.'
I said 'Why?'
He said 'My
dog's died.'

Tommy Cooper

The trees in Siberia are miles apart,
that is why the dogs are so fast.

Bob Hope

———

When it's raining cats and dogs, be
sure not to step in the poodles.

Anonymous

Only mad dogs and
Englishmen go out
in the noonday sun.

Indian proverb

The life of an uneducated man is as useless as the tail of a dog which neither covers its rear end, nor protects it from the bites of insects.

Chanakya

━━◆━━

We see a lot of contestants licking themselves, but we're used to that from covering the Grammys.

Melissa Rivers

━━◆━━

Anybody who doesn't know what soap tastes like never washed a dog.

Franklin P. Jones

Where are the dogs going? ... going
about their business. And they are
very punctilious, without wallets,
notes, and without briefcases.

Charles Baudelaire

Modern houses are so small we've
had to train our dog to wag its tail
up and down and not sideways.

Anonymous

GONE TO THE DOGS

Dogs are a
habit, I think.

Elizabeth Bowen

I had always wanted a dog.
Dogs were freedom, a passport
to running through fields
and staying out all day.

Andrew Dilger, *Dash*

I miss the wagging little tail;
I miss the plaintive, pleading wail;
I miss the wistful, loving glance;
I miss the circling welcome-dance.

Henry Willett, from 'In Memoriam'

[T]he warmly wagging tail of
a dog and the gloriously cold
damp nose... make complete
fools of us human beings.

Barbara Woodhouse

You enter into a certain
amount of madness when you
marry a person with pets.

Nora Ephron

Like two cowboys in a Western, this
dog and I faced each other under
the hot sun. Who would draw first?

Barrie Hawkins

My dogs are a priority and a
big responsibility... but the
payoffs are well worth it.

Will Estes

I'm looking more like my dogs
every day - it must be the
shaggy fringe and the ears.

Christine McVie

Everyone's pet is the
most outstanding.

Jean Cocteau

OLD DOGS AND NEW TRICKS

Old dogs, like old shoes, are comfortable.

Bonnie Wilcox

He's got his dog trained so that
it only does it on newspapers.
The trouble is it does it when
he's reading the blasted things.

Honoré de Balzac

... if you are thinking unpleasant
things about your dog, he will
pick it up and be downhearted.

Barbara Woodhouse

He took to hiding in the
truck, creeping in and trying
to make himself look small.

John Steinbeck on his poodle Charley

Our dog chases
people on a bike.
We've had to
take it off him.

Winston Churchill

When a dog wags her tail and barks at the same time, how do you know which end to believe?

Anonymous

❧

Better not take a dog on the space shuttle, because if he sticks his head out when you're coming home his face might burn up.

Jack Handy

❧

Some of my best leading men have been dogs and horses.

Elizabeth Taylor

I fawn on those who give me anything, I yelp at those who refuse, and I set my teeth in rascals.

Diogenes

❧

Chin on the remote control, belly resting on the newspaper, one eye on the football, the other on my sandwich.

Mark Wallington on how his dog,
Boogie, begs for food

❧

If ever you wanted to see a dog adopting the pose of 'His Master's Voice' with dedicated loyalty, it is Pan when no one is playing darts.

Emma Milne, *Tales from the Tail End*

THE TRUTH ABOUT
MEN AND DOGS

Man is troubled
by... a strange and
involved compulsion
to be as happy and
carefree as a dog.

James Thurber

A dog is not almost-human,
and I know of no greater
insult to the canine race than
to describe it as such.

John Holmes

You can say any fool thing to a dog.

Dave Barry

Most pets display
so many humanlike
traits and emotions it's
easy to forget they're
not gifted with the
English language.

Stephanie Geist

A professor must have a theory
as a dog must have fleas.

H. L. Mencken

❦

I like driving around with my two
dogs... I make them wear little hats
so I can use the car-pool lanes.

Monica Piper

❦

Journalists are like dogs, whenever
anything moves they begin to bark.

Arthur Schopenhauer

Asking a working writer what he thinks about critics is like asking a lamppost how it feels about dogs.

Christopher Hampton

Of one is a greyhound, why try to look like a Pekingese?

Edith Sitwell

Of course his horizons are limited, but how wide are mine?

John Steinbeck on his poodle Charley

I like a bit of mongrel myself,
whether it's a man or a dog.

George Bernard Shaw

❦

A man may smile and bid you hail
Yet wish you to the devil;
But when a good dog wags his tail,
You know he's on the level.

Anonymous

❦

The better I get to know men, the
more I find myself loving dogs.

Charles de Gaulle

CAUTIONARY TAILS

Old age means
realising you will
never own all the
dogs you wanted to.

Joe Gores

Thorns may hurt you, men desert you, sunlight turn to fog; but you're never friendless ever, if you have a dog.

Douglas Mallock

Histories are more full of examples of the fidelity of dogs than of friends.

Alexander Pope

I have caught more ills from people sneezing over me and giving me virus infections than from kissing dogs.

Barbara Woodhouse

The greatness of a Nation and its
moral progress can be judged by
the way its animals are treated.

Mahatma Gandhi

The most affectionate creature
in the world is a wet dog.

Ambrose Bierce

The dogs bark but the
caravan moves on.

Arab proverb

The underdog often starts
the fight, and occasionally the
upper dog deserves to win.

Edgar Watson Howe

Beware of a silent dog
and still water.

Latin proverb

If your dog doesn't like someone
you probably shouldn't either.

Anonymous

What counts is not necessarily the size of the dog in the fight; it's the size of the fight in the dog.

Dwight D. Eisenhower

BAD DOG

Dogs are great.
Bad dogs, if you
can really call them
that, are perhaps the
greatest of them all.

John Grogan

What a dog I got, his favourite
bone is in my arm.

Rodney Dangerfield

When you point out something to
a dog, he looks at your finger.

J. Bryan III

Dogs are lousy poker players.
When they get a good hand
they wag their tails.

Anonymous

He wouldn't hurt a fly, but he has to put up a front because his name's Poppet.

P. G. Wodehouse

Some days you're the dog; some days you're the lamp post.

Anonymous

If it is possible for a dog to have a glint in his eye, then this dog did.

Barrie Hawkins

'Buy one dog, get one flea.'

Sign in pet shop

The sandwich finished, she departed to terrorise the first of many unsuspecting toddlers into parting with their ice creams.

Spud Talbot-Ponsonby, *Two Feet, Four Paws*

Every dog isn't a growler, and every growler isn't a dog.

Anonymous

THE TAIL END

For me a house or an apartment becomes a home when you add one set of four legs...

Roger Caras

Every dog has his day, unless he loses his tail, then he has a weak-end.

June Carter

To a dog the whole world is a smell.

Anonymous

The poor dog, in life
the firmest friend,
The first to welcome,
foremost to defend.

Lord Byron, epitaph for his dog Boatswain

'If you could choose
what to come back as,
what would it be?'
'A dog, so my wife
would love me more.'

Oscar de la Renta, in an interview with *Vanity Fair*

Was there ever a dog that
praised its fleas?

W. B. Yeats

—◆—

The fidelity of a dog is a precious
gift demanding no less binding
moral responsibilities than the
friendship of a human being.

Konrad Lorenz

—◆—

There are three faithful
friends – an old wife, an old
dog and ready money.

Benjamin Franklin

To err is human, to forgive, canine.

Anonymous

Children and dogs are as necessary
to the welfare of the country as
Wall Street and the railroads.

Harry S. Truman

If a dog will not come to you
after having looked you in the
face, you should go home and
examine your conscience.

Woodrow Wilson

Who could not love dogs,
they are such good sports?

Richard Dawkins

To your dog, you are the greatest,
the smartest, the nicest human
being who was ever born.

Louis Sabin

So many get reformed
through religion.
I got reformed
through dogs.

Lina Basquette

If you're interested in finding out more about our humour books, follow us on Twitter: @SummersdaleLOL

www.summersdale.com